Table of Contents

The Velveteen Rabbit

There was once a velveteen rabbit, and
那里 是 曾经 一只 棉绒的 兔子 并且
曾经有

in the beginning he was really splendid. He was fat
在里面 开始 他 是 真的 非常漂亮 他 是 胖的
在最开始

and bunchy, as a rabbit should be; his coat
和 圆润的 就像 一只 兔子 应该 是 他的 外套
就像一只真的兔子一样

was spotted brown and white, he had real thread
是 圆点的 棕色的 和 白色的 他 有 真的 线做的
带有棕色和白色的圆点

whiskers, and his ears were lined with pink sateen.
胡须 并且 他的 耳朵 是被 做内衬 用 粉色的 绵缎
用粉色的绵缎做了衬里

On Christmas morning, when he sat wedged
在 圣诞节的 早晨 当 他 坐在 被楔入

in the top of the Boy's stocking, with
在里面 顶端 男孩的 长筒袜 跟
在……顶端 (有)

a sprig of holly between his paws, the effect was
一个 带叶子的树枝 冬青树 在...之间 他的 前爪 效果 是
一束冬青树枝

charming.
迷人的

There were other things in the stocking, nuts and
那里 有 其他 东西 在...里面 长筒袜 坚果 和

oranges and a toy engine, and chocolate almonds and
橙子 和 一个 玩具 火车头 还有 巧克力 扁桃仁 和

a clockwork mouse, but the Rabbit was
一个 带发条的 老鼠 但是 兔子 是

quite the best of all. For at least two hours the
相当 最好的 所有的 因为 在 最少的 两个 小时
是所有玩具中最好的 至少

Boy loved him, and then Aunts and Uncles
男孩 爱着 他 并且 之后 舅妈 和 舅舅
然后

came to dinner, and there was a great rustling
来 到 晚餐 并且 那里 有 一个 很大的 悉瑟声
来吃晚餐

of tissue paper and unwrapping of parcels, and
（来自） 包装纸 纸 和 打开 包裹 并且

in the excitement of looking at all the new
在…之中 激动的事 看到 所有的 新的

presents the Velveteen Rabbit was forgotten.
礼物 棉绒的 兔子 被 遗忘了

2

Christmas Morning

For a long time he lived in the toy cupboard
经过 一个 长的 时间 他 居住 在...里面 玩具 橱柜
经过了很长的一段时间

or on the nursery floor, and no one
或者 在...上面 保育室 地板 并且 没有 一个
在保育室的地板上 没有人

thought very much about him. He was naturally shy,
想 非常 多 关于 他的 他 是 天生地 羞怯
很想念他

and being only made of velveteen, some of the more
并且 因为是被 只 制作 棉绒 一些 更加
因为他只是由...做成的

expensive toys quite snubbed him. The mechanical toys
昂贵的 玩具 相当 怠慢 他 机械的 玩具

were very superior, and looked down upon
都是 非常 有优越感的 并且 看 低 在...之上
看不起

every one else; they were full of modern ideas, and
所有 一个 其他 他们 是 满的 现代的 主意 并且
其他任何人 充满了

pretended they were real. The model boat, who
假装 他们 是 真的 模型 船 谁

had lived through two seasons and lost most of
生存 通过 两个 季节 并且 丢失了 大多数
已经度过了（此处有一个过去完成时语态）

his paint, caught the tone from them and never
他的 涂料 捕住 语气 从...来 他们 并且 从来不

missed an opportunity of referring to his rigging
错过 一个 机会 涉及 他的 索具
涉及

in technical terms. The Rabbit could not claim to
在...里面 技术的 方面 兔子 能够 不 声称
在技术方面的 不能够

be a model of anything, for he didn't know
(自己)是 一个 模型 任何事 因为 他 不 知道
任何东西的模型

3

that　　　real　rabbits　existed;　he　thought　they
（此处引导一个从句）　真的　兔子　存在　他　以为　他们

were　all　stuffed　with　sawdust　like　himself,　and　he
是　所有的　填充了　用　锯末　就像　他自己　并且　他
　　　都被...塞满了

understood　　that　　sawdust　was　quite　out-of-date　and
理解　　　（引导从句）　锯末　是　非常　过时的　并且

should　never　be　mentioned　in　modern
应该　永远不　被（表示被动语态）　提及　在...里面　时髦的

circles.　Even　Timothy,　the　jointed　wooden　lion,
圈子　甚至　蒂姆森　　关节可以活动的　木头的　狮子

who　　was　made　by　the　disabled　soldiers,　and
谁（引导从句）　（被动语态）　制作　由　　残缺的　士兵　并且
　　　　　　　　被...制作的

should　have　had　broader　views,　put　on　airs　and
应该　　有　更广大的　视野　放在　在...上面　空气　并且
本来应该拥有　　　　　　　　　　摆架子

pretended　he　　was　connected　with　Government.
假装　他　是（被动语态）　有关系　和　政府
　　　　和......有关

Between　them　all　the　poor　little　Rabbit　was　made　to
在...之间　他们　所有的　可怜的　小的　兔子　被　让

feel　himself　very　insignificant　and　commonplace,　and　the
感到　他自己　非常　无关紧要的　并且　平凡的　并且

only　person　who　was　kind　to　him　at　all　was　the
唯一的　人　（引导从句）　是　友好的　对　他　至少一点点　是

Skin　Horse.
皮革　马
皮革制成的马

The Skin Horse had lived longer in the nursery than
皮革 马 生活 更长 在 保育室 比
生活在……的时间更长

any of the others. He was so old that his
任何 的 其他的 他 是 那么 老的 (引导从句) 他的
其他人

brown coat was bald in patches and showed the
棕色的 外套 是 磨光的 补丁 并且 显露出
在有些部分

seams underneath, and most of the hairs in his tail
线缝 在下面 并且 大多数的 毛 在 他的 尾巴
在他的尾巴里

had been pulled out to string bead
已经 被 拉 出来 为了 用（线，链子等）穿起来 珠子
（过去完成时被动语态）已经被

necklaces. He was wise, for he had seen a long
项链 他 是 博学的 因为 他 已经 看过了 一段 长的

succession of mechanical toys arrive to boast and
连串 的 机械的 玩具 到达 然后 自吹自擂 和

swagger, and by-and-by break their mainsprings and
趾高气扬 并且 不久之后 损坏了 他们的 主发条 和

pass away, and he knew that they were only toys,
穿过 离去 并且 他 知道 (引导从句) 他们 是 只是 玩具
去世

and would never turn into anything else. For nursery
并且 将 永远不 转变 进入 任何事 其他的 因为 保育室
变成 任何其他的事

magic is very strange and wonderful, and only those
魔法 是 非常 不可思议的 和 奇妙的 并且 只有 那些

playthings that are old and wise and experienced
玩具 (引导从句) 是 老的 和 睿智的 和 经验丰富的

like the Skin Horse understand all about it.
就像 皮革 马 (才能)理解 一切 关于 它
（保育室魔法）

"What is REAL?" asked the Rabbit one day, when they
什么 是 真的 问了 兔子 一 天 当 他们

were lying side by side near the nursery fender,
是 躺在 旁边 在 旁边 靠近 保育室 挡板
(正在进行时) 正躺在 并排

before Nana came to tidy the room. "Does it mean
在...之前 奶奶 过来 清理 房间 是不是 它 意味着
它是不是

having things that buzz inside you and a
拥有 事物 (引导从句) 嗡嗡声 在...里面 你 和 一个
发出嗡嗡声的东西 在你里面

stick-out handle?"
突出的 把手

"Real isn't how you are made," said the Skin Horse.
真的 不是 如何 你 被 制作的 说了 皮革 吗

"It's a thing that happens to you. When a
是 一种 事情 (引导从句) 发生 对 你 当 一个

child loves you for a long, long time, not just to
孩子 爱 你 一段 长 长的 时间 不是 仅仅 用于

play with, but REALLY loves you, then you become
玩耍 跟(你) 而是 真正的 爱 你 然后 你 变成了

Real."
真的

"Does it hurt?" asked the Rabbit.
是不是 它 疼的 问了 兔子
它会不会

"Sometimes," said the Skin Horse, for he was always
有时　　　说了　　皮革　马　因为　他　是　总是
皮革马说

truthful. "When you are Real you don't mind being
真实的　当　你　是　真的　你　不会　介意　被

hurt."
伤害

"Does it happen all at once, like being wound up," he
是不是　它　发生　都　在　一次　像是　被人　上发条的　他
一下子

asked, "or bit by bit?"
问了　或者　一点　接　一点
逐渐地

"It doesn't happen all at once," said the Skin Horse.
它　不是　发生　都　在　一次　说了　皮革　马
一下子

"You become. It takes a long time. That's why it
你　转变　它　花费　一段　长的　时间　那就是　为什么　他

doesn't happen often to people who break easily,
并不会　发生　通常　在　人　（引倒从句）　损坏　轻易地
轻易损坏的人

or have sharp edges, or who have to be
或者　有　尖锐的　边缘　或者　（引导从句）　需要　被

carefully kept. Generally, by the time you are Real,
小心地　保存　总体上来说　到　时间　你　是　真的
到你是真实的时候

most of your hair has been loved off, and your eyes
大部分　你的　毛发　已经　被　爱　掉了　并且　你的　眼睛
爱抚掉了

drop out and you get loose in the joints and very
落下　出去　并且　你　变得　松脱的　在...里面　关节　并且　非常

7

shabby. But these things don't matter at all, because
破旧的 但是 这些 东西 没 有关系 全部 因为
一点关系也没有

once you are Real you can't be ugly, except to
一旦 你 是 真的 你 不能 是 丑陋的 除了 对

people who don't understand."
人们 （引导从句） 不能 理解
不能理解的人

"I suppose you are real?" said the Rabbit. And then
我 猜想 你 是 真的 说了 兔子 并且 接下来

he wished he had not said it, for
他 希望（不可能实现的愿望） 他 （过去完成时） 从来没有 说 它 因为
这话

he thought the Skin Horse might be sensitive. But the
他 想 皮革 马 也许 会 敏感的 但是

Skin Horse only smiled.
皮革 马 只是 微笑

The Skin Horse Tells His Story

"The Boy's Uncle made me Real," he said. "That was
男孩的 舅舅 让 我 真的 他 说 那 是
让我变成了真的

a great many years ago; but once you are Real you
一个 大量的 许多 年 以前 但是 一旦 你 是 真的 你
很多年以前

can't become unreal again. It lasts for always."
不能够 变成 不真实的 再次 那 持续 到 永远

The Rabbit sighed. He thought it would be a long
兔子 叹气 他 想 那 将会 是 一个 长的

time before this magic called Real happened to
时间 在......之前 这个 魔法 被叫做 真的 发生 到

him. He longed to become Real, to know
他（的身上） 他 渴望 变成 真的 为了 知道

what it felt like; and yet the idea of growing
什么 它 感觉 如何 并且 可是 （这个） 想法 变得
它是什么感觉 （变破旧...）这个想法

shabby and losing his eyes and whiskers was rather
破旧的 和 丢掉 他的 眼睛 和 胡子 是 相当

sad. He wished that he could become it
难过的 他 希望 （引导从句） 他 能够 变成 它
（真的）

without these uncomfortable things happening to
没有 这些 不舒服的 事情 发生 到
（但是不用）

him.
他的（身上）

9

There was a person called Nana who ruled the nursery. Sometimes she took no notice of the playthings lying about, and sometimes, for no reason whatever, she went swooping about like a great wind and hustled them away in cupboards. She called this "tidying up," and the playthings all hated it, especially the tin ones. The Rabbit didn't mind it so much, for wherever he was thrown he came down soft.

One evening, when the Boy was going to bed, he couldn't find the china dog that always slept with him. Nana was in a hurry, and it was too much trouble to hunt for china dogs at bedtime,

10

so she simply looked about her, and seeing that
所以 她 简直 看 四处 她 并且 （当她）看到 （引导从句）
看她周围

the toy cupboard door stood open, she
玩具 橱柜 门 站立 打开 她
开着呢

made a swoop.
做了 一个 突然袭击
迅速走过去抓起来（一个东西）

"Here," she said, "take your old Bunny! He'll do
给 她 说 拿 你的 旧的 兔子 它（能） 行

to sleep with you!" And she dragged the Rabbit out
睡觉 和 你 并且 她 拉了 兔子 出来
陪你一起睡

by one ear, and put him into the Boy's arms.
拿着 一个 耳朵 并且 放置 他 进入 男孩的 胳膊
把他放进

That night, and for many nights after, the Velveteen
那个 夜晚 还有 （持续） 许多 夜晚 之后 棉绒

Rabbit slept in the Boy's bed. At first he found
兔子 睡觉 在 男孩的 床（上） 在 首先 他 发现
最初

it rather uncomfortable, for the Boy hugged
它（和男孩一起睡） 相当 不舒服的 因为 男孩 抱住

him very tight, and sometimes he rolled over on
他 非常 紧的 并且 有时候 他 翻滚 在...上面

him, and sometimes he pushed him so far
他（的身体） 并且 有时候 他 推 他（的身体） 那么 远的

under the pillow that the Rabbit
在...下面 枕头 会引起 兔子

could scarcely breathe. And he missed, too, those long
moonlight hours in the nursery, when all the
house was silent, and his talks with the Skin Horse.
But very soon he grew to like it, for the
Boy used to talk to him, and made nice tunnels for
him under the bedclothes that he said were like
the burrows the real rabbits lived in. And they
had splendid games together, in whispers, when Nana
had gone away to her supper and left the
night-light burning on the mantelpiece. And when
the Boy dropped off to sleep, the Rabbit would
snuggle down close under his little warm chin
and dream, with the Boy's hands clasped close round
him all night long.

And so time went on, and the little Rabbit was
并且 这样 时间 过 下去了 而 小的 兔子 是
而如此 随着时间的推移

very happy - so happy that he never noticed how his
非常 快乐 那么 快乐 他 从未 注意到 如何 他的
太快乐以至于...

beautiful velveteen fur was getting
美丽的 棉绒 皮毛 （正）在 变得

shabbier and shabbier, and his tail becoming
（更加）破旧的 而 （更加）破旧的 并且 他的 尾巴 变得
越来越破旧的

unsewn, and all the pink rubbed off his nose
缝线被拆开的 并且 所有的 粉色 摩擦 脱落 他的 鼻子
擦掉

where the Boy had kissed him.
在...的地方 男孩 亲吻 他
在男孩亲他的那些地方

Spring came, and they had long days in the garden,
春天 来了 并且 他们 拥有了 悠长的 日子 在 花园（里）

for wherever the Boy went the Rabbit went too. He
因为 不管在哪里 男孩 去了 兔子 去了 也 他
也去了

had rides in the wheelbarrow, and picnics on the
有了 旅程 在 独轮手推车 并且 野餐 在
乘坐了

grass, and lovely fairy huts built for him under the
草地（上） 并且 可爱的 纤巧的 小屋 被建造 为了 他 在...下面

raspberry canes behind the flower border. And once,
树莓的 藤条 在 花朵的 边缘（后面） 还有 一次

when the Boy was called away suddenly to go out
当 男孩 被 呼叫 离开 突然间 为了 去 外面
叫走

to tea, the Rabbit was left out on the lawn until
去 （喝）茶 兔子 被 遗落在 外面 在 草坪（上） 直到
遗漏

13

long after dusk, and Nana had to come and
长（时间）的 在...之后 黄昏 并且 奶奶 不得不 来 而
黄昏到了很久之后

look for him with the candle because the Boy couldn't
寻找 他 拿着 蜡烛 因为 男孩 不能够

go to sleep unless he was there. He was
去 睡觉 除非 他 在 那里 他 被
（代指兔子）

wet through with the dew and quite earthy from
打湿 穿过 （因为） 露水 和 非常 有泥土味的 因为
露水湿透了

diving into the burrows the Boy had made for him
潜水 进去 （那些） 地洞 男孩 曾经 制作 给 他
投入

in the flower bed, and Nana grumbled as she
在...里面 花 床 而 奶奶 （一边）抱怨 一边 她
花坛

rubbed him off with a corner of her apron.
摩擦 他 出来 用 一 角 她的 围裙
把他擦掉

Spring Time

"You must have your old Bunny!" she said. "Fancy
你 必须 有 你的 旧的 兔子 她 说了 想象

all that fuss for a toy!"
所有的 那个 小题大做 为了 一个 玩具
那么多

The Boy sat up in bed and stretched out his
男孩 坐了 起来 在…里面 床 并且 张开 出来 他的
伸出

hands.
双手

"Give me my Bunny!" he said. "You mustn't say
给 我 我的 兔子 他 说了 你 一定不能 说

that. He isn't a toy. He's REAL!"
那个 他 并不是 一个 玩具 他是 真的
(那样的话)

When the little Rabbit heard that he was happy,
当 小的 兔子 听到 那(句话) 他 是 开心的

for he knew that
因为 他 知道 (引导从句)

what the Skin Horse had said was true at last.
什么 皮革 马 曾经 说过(的) 是 真的 最后
皮革马说过的话

The nursery magic had happened to him, and he
保育室的 魔法 已经 发生了 到 他的(身上) 并且 他

was a toy no longer. He was Real. The Boy himself
是 一个 玩具 不 更长 他 是 真的 男孩 自己
再也不是了

had said it.
已经 说了 它

That night he was almost too happy to sleep, and
那个 夜晚 他 是 几乎 太 高兴 （没能） 睡觉 并且
太开心了以至于没能……

so much love stirred in his little sawdust heart
那么 多 爱情 搅动 在 他的 小的 锯木屑 心脏（里）

that it almost burst. And into his boot-button
（以至于）它 差点就 爆炸了 并且 在…里面 他的 靴子纽扣一样的
（他的心脏）

eyes, that had long ago lost their polish, there
眼睛 （引导从句）已经很久之前 失去了 他们的 光彩 那里

came a look of wisdom and beauty, so that even
来了 一个 …的样子 智慧 和 美丽 以至于 甚至

Nana noticed it next morning when she
奶奶 注意到了 它 下一个 早晨 当 她

picked him up, and said, "I declare
选择 他 起来 并且 说了 我 声明
捡起他了 真有点奇怪啊

if that old Bunny hasn't got quite a knowing
如果 那个 旧 兔子 没 有 非常 一个 （看起来）有见识的
真好像那只兔子有

expression!"
表情

That was a wonderful Summer!
那 是 一个 非常棒的 夏天

16

Near the house where they lived there was a
靠近 房子 （引导从句） 他们 住着的 那 是 一片
他们住的房子 有

wood, and in the long June evenings the Boy liked
树林 并且 在…里面 漫长的 六月的 晚上 男孩 喜欢

to go there after tea to play. He took the Velveteen
去 那里 在…之后 午茶 玩 他 带着 棉绒

Rabbit with him, and before he wandered off to pick
兔子 和 他 并且 在…之前 他 漫步 下去 为了 采摘
走散

flowers, or play at brigands among the trees, he
花朵 或者 玩耍 在 土匪 在 树 （之间） 他
玩一个设想自己是土匪的游戏

always made the Rabbit a little nest somewhere
总是 制作 （给）兔子 一个 小的 窝 在某个地方

among the bracken, where he would be quite cosy,
在 欧洲蕨 （之间） （引导从句） 他 会 是 相当 舒适的

for he was a kind-hearted little boy and he liked
因为 他 是 一个 有爱心的 小的 男孩 并且 他 喜欢

Bunny to be comfortable. One evening, while the
兔子 是 舒适的 一个 晚上 当

Rabbit was lying there alone, watching the ants
兔子 正 躺在 那里 一个人 看着 蚂蚁

that ran to and fro between his velvet paws
（引导从句） 跑 进 和 向后 在 他的 棉绒 爪子 （之间）
跑来跑去

in the grass, he saw two strange beings creep
在…里面 草丛 他 看到了 两个 奇怪的 生物 蹑手蹑脚地移动

out of the tall bracken near him.
从…出来 高的 欧洲蕨 靠近 他的

They were rabbits like himself, but quite furry and
他们 是 兔子 就像 他自己（一样） 但是 非常 毛茸茸的 和

brand-new. They must have been very well made, for
崭新的 他们 一定 （过去式） 被 非常 好地 制作 因为

their seams didn't show at all, and they changed
他们的 线缝 没有 显露出来 在 所有的 并且 他们 改变了
完全没有显露出来

shape in a queer way when they moved; one
形状 在...里面 一个 奇怪的 方式 当 他们 移动（的时候） 一
用一种奇怪的方式

minute they were long and thin and the next minute
分钟 他们 是 长的 和 瘦的 接着 下 一分钟

fat and bunchy, instead of always staying the
（变成）胖的 和 圆润的 而不是 总是 保持

same like he did. Their feet padded softly on
同样的（状态） 像 他 做的（那样） 他们的 双脚 轻轻的走 柔软地 在

the ground, and they crept quite close to him,
地上 并且 他们 蹑手蹑脚地移动 非常 靠近 他
他们悄悄走到非常靠近他的位置

twitching their noses, while the Rabbit stared hard to
抽动着 他们的 鼻子 当 兔子 盯着看 努力地 为了

see which side the clockwork stuck out, for he knew
看到 （从）哪 边 发条 插 出来了 因为 他 知道
突出

that people who jump generally have something
（引导从句） 人们 （引导从句） 跳跃的 通常 有 一些

to wind them up. But he couldn't see it. They
要 给...上发条 他们 起来 但是 他 不能够 看到 它 他们
给他们上发条

were evidently a new kind of rabbit altogether.
是 显然地 一种 新的 种类 兔子 全然
完全新的一种类兔子

Summer Days

They stared at him, and the little Rabbit stared back.
他们 盯着看 对 他 并且 小的 兔子 盯着看 回去
凝视

And all the time their noses twitched.
并且 所有的 时间 他们的 鼻子 抽动着
一直

"Why don't you get up and play with us?"
为什么 不 你 起床 并且 玩耍 和 我们
你为什么不

one of them asked.
一个 他们 问了
他们中的一个

"I don't feel like it," said the Rabbit, for he didn't
我 (就是)不 感觉 喜欢 那样 说了 兔子 因为 他 不
想 (做某事)

want to explain that he had no clockwork.
想要 解释 (引导从句) 他 有 没 发条
没有

"Ho!" said the furry rabbit. "It's as easy as anything,"
呼呼 说了 毛茸茸的 兔子 那 像 容易 像 任何东西
像...一样容易

And he gave a big hop sideways and
并且 他 给了 一个 大的 跳跃 斜向一边地 并且

stood on his hind legs.
站着 在...上面 他的 后部的 腿
用他的后腿站立

"I don't believe you can!" he said.
我 不 相信 你 能 他 说了

"I can!" said the little Rabbit. "I can jump higher
我   可以   说了   小的   兔子   我 可以   跳   更高

than anything!" He meant when the Boy threw
比   任何东西   他 指的是   当   男孩   扔

him, but of course he didn't want to say so.
他（的时候）但是 当然   他   不   想   说 这个
                                    并不想这样说

"Can you hop on your hind legs?" asked the furry
可以 你   跳跃 用 你的 后面的 腿   问了   毛茸茸的
你可以…吗？   用你的后腿跳

rabbit.
兔子

That was a dreadful question, for the Velveteen
那   是 一个 糟糕透顶的   问题   因为   棉绒

Rabbit had no hind legs at all! The back of him
兔子   有 没 后部的 腿 所有的   后背   他的
              根本没有后腿   他的后面

was made all in one piece, like a pincushion. He
被   制作 都 在 一个 块   像 一个 针垫   他
              都是一块

sat still in the bracken, and hoped that the other
坐着 不动的 在 欧洲蕨（里）并且 希望 （引导从句） 另外的

rabbits wouldn't notice.
兔子们   不会   注意到

"I don't want to!" he said again.
我 不   想要 （做那个）他 说了 再一次

But the wild rabbits have very sharp eyes. And this
但是 这 野生的 兔子们 拥有 非常 锐利的 眼睛 并且 这

one stretched out his neck and looked.
一个 伸展 出 他的 脖子 并且 看到
　　　　伸出

"He hasn't got any hind legs!" he called out. "Fancy
他 没有 任何 后部的 腿 他 呼叫 出来 想象一下
　　　　　　　　　　　　　　　 大声叫唤

a rabbit without any hind legs!" And he began to
一只 兔子 （居然）没有 任何 后部的 腿 并且 他 开始

laugh.
大笑

"I have!" cried the little Rabbit. "I have got hind
我 有 哭了 小的 兔子 我 有 后部的

legs! I am sitting on them!"
腿 我 正在 坐着 在 他们（上面）

"Then stretch them out and show me, like this!"
那么 伸出 它们 出来 并且 展示（给） 我 像 这样
　　 把它们伸出来

said the wild rabbit. And he began to whirl round
说了 这 野生的 兔子 并且 他 开始 迅速旋转 围绕

and dance, till the little Rabbit got quite dizzy.
和 跳舞 直到 小的 兔子 （感到） 非常 头晕目眩的

"I don't like dancing," he said. "I'd rather sit still!"
我 不 喜欢 跳舞 他 说了 我 宁愿 坐 不动

21

But all the while he was longing to dance, for a
但是 全部 一段时间 他 是 渴望 跳舞 因为 一个
一直

funny new tickly feeling ran through him, and he
难以解释的 新的 让人发痒的 感觉 跑 穿过 他 并且 他
穿过

felt he would give anything in the world to
感觉 他 将会 给予 任何事物 在 世界（上） 为了

be able to jump about like these rabbits did.
能够 跳来跳去 像...一样 那些 兔子 做的

The strange rabbit stopped dancing, and came quite
奇怪的 兔子 停止 跳舞 并且 走过来 非常的

close. He came so close this time that his long
靠近 他 走过来 那么 近 这 次 以至于 他的 长的

whiskers brushed the Velveteen Rabbit's ear, and then
胡子 刷到了 棉绒 兔子的 耳朵 并且 接下来

he wrinkled his nose suddenly and flattened his ears
他 皱起 他的 鼻子 突然地 并且 （使）变平 他的 耳朵

and jumped backwards.
并且 跳了 向后

"He doesn't smell right!" he exclaimed. "He
他 不 闻起来 对的 他 惊呼了 他
他闻起来（的味道）不对

isn't a rabbit at all! He isn't real!"
不是 一只 兔子 全部 他 不是 真的
根本不是一只兔子

22

"I am Real!" said the little Rabbit. "I am Real! The
我 是 真的 说了 小的 兔子 我 是 真的

Boy said so!" And he nearly began to cry.
男孩 说了 (是)这样的 并且 他 差点 开始 哭(起来)

Just then there was a sound of footsteps, and the
恰好 那时 那里 有 一个 声音 脚步 并且
正当那时 脚步声

Boy ran past near them, and with a stamp of feet
男孩 跑 过去 接近 他们 并且 伴随着 一串 踩 脚
伴随着遗传脚步声

and a flash of white tails the two strange rabbits
和 一道 闪光 白色的 尾巴 两只 奇怪的 兔子

disappeared.
消失了

"Come back and play with me!" called the little
来 回来 并且 玩 和 我 叫着 小的
回来

Rabbit. "Oh, do come back! I know I am Real!"
兔子 哦 真的 来 回来 我 知道 我 是 真的

But there was no answer, only the little ants
但是 那里 是 没有 回答 只有 小的 蚂蚁
没有

ran to and fro, and the bracken swayed gently
跑 进 和 向后 还有 欧洲蕨 摇摆 轻柔地
跑来跑去

where the two strangers had passed. The
在(引导从句) 两只 陌生(兔子) 刚才 穿过的(地方)

Velveteen Rabbit was all alone.
棉绒 兔子 是 完全的 孤独的
独自地

"Oh, dear!" he thought. "Why did they run away like
噢　天啊　他　想　为什么　他们　跑　离开　就像
　　　　　　　　　　　　　　　　跑开

that? Why couldn't they stop and talk to me?"
那样　为什么　不能　他们　停下来　并且　谈话　和　我

For a long time he lay very still, watching the
持续　一段　很长的　时间　他　躺着　非常　不动　看着
　　很长时间　　　　　　他一动不动地躺着

bracken, and hoping that they would come back.
欧洲蕨　并且　希望　（引导从句）　他们　会　来　回来
　　　　　　　　　　　　　　　　　　回来

But they never returned, and presently the sun sank
但是　他们　再也没有　返回　并且　现在　太阳　下沉

lower and the little white moths fluttered out, and the
更低　并且　小的　白色的　飞蛾　拍打（翅膀）　出来　并且

Boy came and carried him home.
男孩　来了　并且　抱（着）　他　（回）家

Weeks passed, and the little Rabbit grew very old
数周　过去了　并且　小的　兔子　渐渐变得　非常　旧的

and shabby, but the Boy loved him just as much.
和　肮脏破旧的　但是　男孩　爱　他　仅仅　跟...一样　大量的
　　　　　　　　　　　　　　　　还是像原来一样多

He loved him so hard that he
他　爱　他　那么　用力地　以致于　他

loved all his whiskers off, and the pink
爱　所有　他的　胡子　掉落　并且　粉色的
爱得让他胡子都掉落了

lining to his ears turned grey, and his brown spots
衬里　为　他的　耳朵　变得　灰色　并且　他的　棕色的　斑点
他耳朵的衬里

faded. He even began to lose his shape, and he
褪色了　他　甚至　开始　　　失去　他的　形状　并且　他

scarcely looked like a rabbit any more, except to the
几乎不　看起来　像　一只　兔子　不再...了　除了　对

Boy. To him he was always beautiful, and that
男孩（来说）对　他（来说）他　是　永远　漂亮的　并且　那

was all that the little Rabbit cared about. He
是　所有的　（引导从句）　小的　兔子　在乎　关于　他
　　　　　　小兔子在乎的一切

didn't mind how he looked to other people, because
不　介意　如何　他　看起来　对　其他的　人　因为

the nursery magic had made him Real, and when
保育室　魔法　已经　让　他（变成）真的　并且　当

you are Real shabbiness doesn't matter.
你　是　真的　破旧不堪　没有　关系

And then, one day, the Boy was ill.
然后　（有）一　天　男孩　是　生病的

His face grew very flushed, and he
他的　脸蛋　渐渐变得　很　潮红　并且　他

talked in his sleep, and his little body was so hot
说话　在　他的　睡眠　并且　他的　小的　身体　是　那么　热的
　　　说梦话了

that it burned the Rabbit when he held him
以致于　它　烫到　兔子　当　他　抱着　他
　　　（代指他的身体）

close. Strange people came and went in the nursery,
紧靠着　陌生的　人们　进来　又　出去　在　保育室

and a light burned all night and through it all
并且 一盏 灯 燃烧 整个 夜晚 并且 穿过 它 全部的
当这一切在发生的时候

the little Velveteen Rabbit lay there, hidden from sight
小的 棉绒 兔子 躺在 那里 藏在 来自于 视线
躲藏在视线之外

under the bedclothes, and he never stirred, for he
在……下面 床上用品 他 从未 移动 因为 他
在被子底下

was afraid that if they found him some one
害怕 （引导从句） 如果 他们 发现了 他 某 人

might take him away, and he knew that the Boy
可能会 带 他 走 并且 他 知道 （引导从句） 男孩

needed him.
需要 他

It was a long weary time, for the Boy was too
它 是 一段 漫长的 令人疲倦的 时光 因为 男孩 是 太

ill to play, and the little Rabbit found it
病的严重 以至于不能 玩 并且 小的 兔子 发现

rather dull with nothing to do all day long. But he
相当的 沉闷的 没有任何事 做 整个 一天 长 但是 他
整天无事可做

snuggled down patiently, and looked forward to the
依偎 下来 有耐心地 并且 看 向前 那个
舒适得依偎着 期待

time when the Boy should be well again, and they
时候 当 男孩 应该 痊愈 再次 而（那时） 他们

would go out in the garden amongst the flowers and
将会 走 出去 在 花园（里面） 在…中间 花朵 和

the butterflies and play splendid games in the
蝴蝶 并且 玩 极好的 游戏 在

raspberry thicket like they used to. All sorts of
树莓 丛（里面）就像 他们 以前 （做过的那样） 所有 类型的

delightful things he planned, and while the Boy lay
令人愉快的 事物 他 计划了 而且 在...期间 男孩 躺着

half asleep he crept up close to the pillow and
一半 入睡 他 小心行进 上 靠近 枕头 并且

whispered them in his ear. And presently the
小声说 它们（他的计划）在 他的 耳朵(里面) 并且 不久

fever turned, and the Boy got better. He was able to
高烧 转变 并且 男孩 变得 比以前好 他 能够
（退了） 好起来了

sit up in bed and look at picture-books, while the
坐 起来 在 床(上) 并且 看 图画书 在...时候

little Rabbit cuddled close at his side. And one day,
小的 兔子 拥抱 紧靠 在 他的 旁边 而 一 天

they let him get up and dress.
他们 让 他 起床 并且 穿衣服

It was a bright, sunny morning, and the
（那）是 一个 明亮的 晴朗的 早晨 并且

windows stood wide open. They had carried the Boy
窗户 站立 宽阔的 打开 他们 已经 搬运 男孩
窗户大开

out on to the balcony, wrapped in a shawl, and
出来 在...上面 到 阳台 包裹 在 一条 披肩（里）并且

the little Rabbit lay tangled up among the bedclothes,
小的 兔子 躺着 缠绕在一起 在...之间 床上用品

thinking.
想着

The Boy was going to the seaside to-morrow.
男孩　　是　　要去　　　　　海边　　明天

Everything was arranged, and now it only remained to
所有的事情　被　安排（好）了　而　现在　它　只　剩下了

carry out the doctor's orders. They
携带　出去　　　　医生的　　命令　　他们
执行

talked about it all, while the little Rabbit lay under
谈论过　关于　它的　一切　　在　　小的　兔子　躺着　在
全部都谈论过了

the bedclothes, with just his head peeping out,
床上用品（下面的时候）　跟　仅仅　他的　脑袋　隐约可见　出来
只有　　　　　　　　　　　　露出

and listened. The room was to be disinfected, and
并且　听到　　房间　　将要被　　给消毒的　并且

all the books and
所有的　　　　书籍　　　和

toys that the Boy had played with in bed must
玩具　（引导从句）　男孩　以前　玩耍　和　在　床（上）　必须
　　　　男孩玩耍过的玩具

be burnt.
被　焚毁

"Hurrah!" thought the little Rabbit. "To-morrow we
（欢呼）好极了　想着　　小的　兔子　　明天　我们

shall go to the seaside!" For the boy had often
将要　去　到　　海边　　因为　　男孩　以前　经常

talked of the seaside, and he wanted very much to
谈话　说到　海边　并且　他　想　非常　多
说到　　　　　　　　　　　非常想

see the big waves coming in, and the tiny crabs,
看到 大的 海浪 （涌）过来 还有 微小的 螃蟹

and the sand castles.
和 沙子 城堡

Just then Nana caught sight of him.
仅仅 那时 奶奶 抓到 视线 他
就在那时 看到

"How about his old Bunny?" she asked.
... ...呢？ 他的 旧的 兔子 她 问了
那他的旧兔子呢？

"That?" said the doctor. "Why, it's a mass of
那个 说 医生 啊呀！ 那是 一 堆

scarlet fever germs! -Burn it at once. What? Nonsense!
猩红色的 高烧 细菌 烧掉 它 在 一次 什么 胡说
猩红热的 立刻

Get him a new one. He mustn't have that
给 他 一个 新 的（兔子） 他 一定不能 拥有 那个

any more!"
了

Anxious Times

And so the little Rabbit was put into a sack
而　　这样　　　　小的　　兔子　　被　　放置　　到　　一个　　麻布袋（里）

with the old picture-books and a lot of rubbish, and
跟　　旧的　　图画书　　　　和　　　许多的　　　垃圾　　并且

carried out to the end of the garden behind the
抬　　出去　　到　　　尽头　　　　　花园　　在…后面
　　　　　　　　　花园的尽头

fowl-house. That was a fine place to make a
鸡窝　　　那　　是　　一个　　很好的　　地方　　为了　　制作　　一个

bonfire, only the gardener was too busy just then to
火堆　　只不过　　　　园丁　　是　　太　　忙碌的　　仅仅　　那时

attend to it. He had the potatoes to dig and the
照料　　它　　他　有　　　　土豆　　（需要）去　挖　　还有

green peas to gather, but next morning he
绿色的　　豌豆　（需要）去　收获　　但是　　第二天　　早晨　　他

promised to come quite early and burn the whole
承诺　　（会）　来（到花园）　非常　　早　　并且　烧掉　　　所有的

lot.
一堆

That night the Boy slept in a different bedroom, and
那个　　晚上　　　男孩　睡　　在　一个　　不同的　　　卧室　　并且

he had a new bunny to sleep with him. It was a
他　有了　一个　新的　兔子　　睡觉　和　他　　那　是　一个

splendid bunny, all white plush with real glass eyes,
漂亮的　　兔子　　所有的　白色的　容貌　和　　真的　玻璃　眼睛

but the Boy was too excited to care very much
但是 男孩 是 太 激动 以至于不能 在乎 很 多

about it. For to-morrow he was going to the seaside,
关于 它 因为 明天 他 将要 去 海边

and that in itself was such a wonderful thing that
并且 那 在...里面 它自己 是 那么 个 极好的 事情 以至于
本身

he could think of nothing else.
他 能够 想到 没有任何事 其他的
想不到任何其他的事情

And while the Boy was asleep, dreaming of the
而 当 男孩 在 睡觉 在梦 到

seaside, the little Rabbit lay among the old
海边 小的 兔子 躺 在...之间 旧的

picture-books in the corner behind the fowl-house, and
图画书（之间） 在 角落 在...后面 鸡窝 并且
在鸡窝后面的角落

he felt very lonely. The sack had been left
他 感到 非常 孤独 （装着兔子的） 麻布袋 被 留了

untied, and so by wriggling a bit he was able to
没有系好的 并且 所以 靠 扭动 一 点儿 他 能够

get his head through the opening and look out. He
使得 他的 头 通过 打开的（袋口） 并且 看 出 他
看向外面

was shivering a little, for he had always
在 发抖 一 点儿 因为 他 （以前） 一直

been used to sleeping in a proper bed, and
习惯于 睡 在 一个 合适的 床 并且

by this time his coat had worn so thin and
到 这个 时间 他的 外套 已经 穿着 非常 薄的 并且
到现在

threadbare from hugging that it was no longer any
破旧的 因为 拥抱 以致于 它 是 不 再 任何
不再有

protection to him. Near by he could see
保护 对 他 在附近 他 能够 看见

the thicket of raspberry canes, growing tall and close
树丛 树莓 藤条 生长得 高的 并且 紧挨的
树梅丛

like a tropical jungle, in whose shadow he had
像 一个 热带 丛林 在 (树莓丛的) 树荫（下） 他 曾经

played with the Boy on bygone mornings. He thought
玩耍 和 男孩 在 过去了的 早晨 他 想
和…一起玩耍

of those long sunlit hours in the garden-
到 那些 漫长的 阳光普照的 时刻 在 花园

how happy they were –and a great sadness
多么 开心 他们 是 然后 一阵 巨大的 悲伤
他们当时有多么开心！

came over him. He seemed to see them all pass
来 过 他 他 似乎 看到 他们 所有 过往
突然产生

before him, each more beautiful than the other, the
在…之前 他 每一个 更加 漂亮 比 其他的 上一个
在他眼前 上一个

fairy huts in the flower-bed, the quiet evenings in the
纤巧的 小屋 在 花床 宁静的 夜晚 在

wood when he lay in the bracken and the little ants
树林 当 他 躺 在 欧洲蕨 和 小的 蚂蚁

ran over his paws; the wonderful day when he first
跑着 越过 他的 爪子 美好的 日子 当 他 第一次

knew that he was Real. He thought of the Skin
知道 (引导从句) 他 是 真的 他 想 到 皮革

Horse, so wise and gentle, and all that he had
马 那么 聪慧 和 温和 还有 所有的 (引导从句) 他 曾经

told him. Of what use was it to be loved and lose one's beauty and become Real if it all ended like this? And a tear, a real tear, trickled down his little shabby velvet nose and fell to the ground.

And then a strange thing happened. For where the tear had fallen a flower grew out of the ground, a mysterious flower, not at all like any that grew in the garden. It had slender green leaves the colour of emeralds, and in the centre of the leaves a blossom like a golden cup. It was so beautiful that the little Rabbit forgot to cry, and just lay there watching it. And presently the blossom opened, and out of it there stepped a fairy.

She was quite the loveliest fairy in the whole world.
她　是　相当的　最可爱的　仙女　在　整个　世界（上）

Her dress was of pearl and dew-drops, and there
她的　裙子　是　用　珍珠　和　露珠（做的）　并且　那里（仙女身上）

were flowers round her neck and in her hair, and
有　花朵　围绕着　她的　脖子　和　在　她的　头发（里）　并且

her face was like the most perfect flower of all.
她的　脸蛋　很　像　最　完美的　花朵　所有的
所有花之中

And she came close to the little Rabbit and
接着　她　来　近　到　小的　兔子　并且

gathered him up in her arms and kissed him on
收集　他　起　在　她的　胳膊（里）　并且　亲吻了　他　在
把他收集起来

his velveteen nose that was
他的　棉绒的　鼻子（上面）　（引导从句）　是

all damp from crying.
全部　便潮湿　因为　哭泣
全部因为哭泣而变得潮湿

"Little Rabbit," she said, "don't you know who I am?"
小的　兔子　她　说　不　你　知道　谁　我　是
你不知道我是谁吗？

The Rabbit looked up at her, and it seemed to him
兔子　看　起来　向　她　并且　似乎　对　他
抬起头看她

that he had seen her face before, but he couldn't
（引导从句）　他　曾经　见过　她的　脸　以前　但是　他　不能

think where.
想起　在哪里

"I am the nursery magic Fairy," she said. "I
我 是 保育室 魔法 仙女 她 说了 我

take care of all the playthings that the children
照顾 所有的 玩具 （引导从句） 孩子们

have loved. When they are old and worn out and the
曾经 爱过的 当 他们 是 旧的 和 用坏了的 并且

children don't need them any more, then I come and
孩子们 不 需要 他们 了 那时 我 过来 并且

take them away with me and turn them into Real."
带 他们 离开 和 我 并且 转变 他们 成为 真的
把他们变成

"Wasn't I Real before?" asked the little Rabbit.
不是 我 真的 之前 问了 小的 兔子
我之前不是真的吗？

"You were Real to the Boy," the Fairy said, "because
你 是 真的 对于 男孩 仙女 说了 因为

he loved you. Now you shall be Real to every one."
他 爱 你 现在 你 可以 成为 真的 对 每 一个人

The Fairy Flower

And she held the little Rabbit close in her arms
并且 她 抱住 小的 兔子 靠近 在 她的 胳膊（里）

and flew with him into the wood.
并且 飞 和 他 进入 森林

It was light now, for the moon had risen. All the
它 是 明亮的 现在 因为 月亮 已经 升起来了 所有的
现在是明亮的

forest was beautiful, and the fronds of the bracken
森林 （都）是 漂亮的 并且 叶子 欧洲蕨
欧洲蕨的叶子

shone like frosted silver. In the open glade
发光 像是 磨砂的 银器 在 开阔的 林间空地

between the tree-trunks the wild rabbits danced with
在...之间 树干 野生的 兔子们 跳舞 和
在树干之间

their shadows on the velvet grass, but when they saw
他们的 影子 在 天鹅绒 草地上 但是 当 他们 看到

the Fairy they all stopped dancing and
仙女 他们 全部都 停止 跳舞 并且

stood round in a ring to stare at her.
站（成） 圆形的 在 一个 环 为了 注视着 她
站成一个圆环形

"I've brought you a new playfellow," the Fairy
我 带来了 （给）你们 一个 新的 玩伴 仙女

said. "You must be very kind to him and teach him
说了 你们 必须 非常 友好的 对 他 并且 教 他

all he needs to know in Rabbit-land, for he is
所有的 他 需要 知道（的） 在 兔子乐园 因为 他

going to live with you for ever and ever!"
将要 生活 和 你们 永远永远

And she kissed the little Rabbit again and
接着 她 亲吻了 小的 兔子 再一次 然后

put him down on the grass.
放置 他 下来 在 草地（上）
把他放下来

"Run and play, little Rabbit!" she said.
跑 和 玩 小的 兔子 她 说

But the little Rabbit sat quite still for a moment
但是 小的 兔子 坐着 非常的 安静的 持续 一 片刻
一会儿

and never moved. For when he saw all the wild
并且 从未 移动过 因为 当 他 看到 所有的 野生的

rabbits dancing around him he suddenly remembered
兔子们 跳舞 围绕 他 他 突然间 想起
围绕着他跳舞

about his hind legs, and he didn't want them to see
到 他的 后部的 腿 并且 他 不 想 他们 看到

that he was made all in one piece. He did not
（引导从句） 他 被 制作 全部 用 一 块（材料） 他 不
都是一块

know that when the Fairy kissed him that last
知道 （引导从句） 当 仙女 亲吻 他 那 最后

time she had changed him altogether. And he
一次（的时候） 她 已经 改变 他 完全 并且 他

might have sat there a long time, too shy to
可能　　会　　坐在　那里　一段　长的　时间　太　害羞　以至于不能

move, if just then something hadn't tickled his nose,
移动　如果　仅仅　那时　某些东西　没有　挠痒　他的　鼻子
　　　　　当口

and before he thought what he was doing he lifted
而　在...之前　他　想　什么　他　在　做　他　举起了
　　　　　　　　　　　　他在做什么

his hind toe to scratch it.
他的　后部的　脚趾　为了　挠　它（痒的鼻子）

And he found that he actually had hind legs!
并且　他　发现　（引导从句）　他　实际上　有了　后部的　腿

Instead of dingy velveteen he had brown fur, soft
代替了　阴暗脏脏的　棉绒　他　拥有了　棕色的　皮毛　（又）柔软的

and shiny, his ears twitched by themselves, and his
又　有光泽的　他的　耳朵　抽动　依靠　他们自己　并且　他的
　　　　　　　　依靠自己就可以抽动

whiskers were so long that they brushed the grass.
胡须　是　那么　长的　以至于　他们　刷过　草地

He gave one leap and
他　给了　一个　跳跃　并且

the joy of using those hind legs was so great that
快乐　使用　那双　后部的　腿　是　那么　棒的　以至于
　　　使用那双后腿的快乐

he went springing about the turf on them, jumping
他　走到　弹起　到处　（在）草皮　在　它们　跳跃
　　　　　　　　　　　　　　（他的腿上）

sideways and whirling round as the others did,
斜向一边地　和　迅速旋转　围绕　像　其他（兔子）做的（一样）
　　　　　　　迅速转圈

and he grew so excited that when at last he
并且 他 渐渐变得 那么 兴奋的 以致于 当...的时候 在 最后 他

did stop to look for the Fairy she had gone.
（终于） 停下来了 为了 寻找 仙女 她 已经 走了

He was a Real Rabbit at last, at home with the
他 是 一只 真的 兔子 在 最后 在 家 和
　　　　　　　　　　　　　　　最终　　　很舒适的

other rabbits.
其他的 兔子（在一起）

At Last! At Last!

Autumn passed and Winter, and in the Spring, when
秋天　　过去了　接着　冬天（来到了）　接着　在　　春天　　当
秋去冬来

the days grew warm and sunny, the Boy went out
天气　渐渐变得　温暖的　和　晴朗的　　男孩　走　出去

to play in the wood behind the house. And while
为了　玩　在...里面　树林　在......后面　房子　并且　当
在房子后面的树林里

he was playing, two rabbits crept out from the
他　正在　玩耍（的时候）　两只　兔子　悄悄移动　出来　从

bracken and peeped at him. One of them was brown
欧洲蕨　并且　偷看　向　他　一个　他们　是　棕色的
他们中的一个

all over, but the other had strange markings under
全部　从头到尾　但是　其他的　有　奇怪的　标记　在...下面

his fur, as though long ago he had been spotted, and
他的　皮毛　就像　长的　以前　他　曾经　是　满是斑点的　并且
很久以前

the spots still showed through. And about his little
斑点　仍然　展示　通过　并且　关于　他的　小小的
穿过（毛皮）可以被看见

soft nose and his round black eyes there was
柔软的　鼻子　和　他的　圆圆的　黑色的　眼睛　有着

something familiar, so that the Boy thought to himself:
一些东西　熟悉的　所以　男孩　想到　他自己
心中想起

"Why, he looks just like my old Bunny that was
啊呀　他　看起来　就　像　我的　旧的　兔子　（引导从句）　被

lost when I had scarlet fever!"
丢失　当　我　得了　猩红的　高烧
猩红热

But he never knew that it really was his own
但是 他 永远不 知道 （引导从句） 他 真的 是 他的 自己的

Bunny, come back to look at the child who had
兔子 来 回来 为了 看 向 孩子 谁（引导从句） 曾经

first helped him to be Real.
第一次 帮助过 他 成为 真的
在最开始